C

Love Songs of the New Kingdom

Illustrated with hieroglyphs drawn by the translator

and with paintings from Egyptian tombs by Nina M. Davies

LOVE SONGS
OF THE
NEW KINGDOM

TRANSLATED FROM THE ANCIENT EGYPTIAN BY

John L. Foster

CHARLES SCRIBNER'S SONS · NEW YORK

Library of Congress Cataloging in Publication Data
Foster, John L   comp.
     Love songs of the New Kingdom.

     CONTENTS: Some rather lively lines (Papyrus Chester Beatty I)—Songs inscribed on an earthen vessel (Cairo ostracon 25218)—Songs of the garden (Papyrus Harris 500) [etc.]
     1. Egyptian poetry—Translations into English.
     2. English poetry—Translations from Egyptian. 3. Love poetry. I. Title.
     PJ1945.F6   893'.1   73-19274
     ISBN 0-684-13781-X

1 3 5 7 9 11 13 15 17 19 Q/C 20 18 16 14 12 10 8 6 4 2

PRINTED IN THE UNITED STATES OF AMERICA

TITLE-PAGE ILLUSTRATION: *A procession of geese*

FOR GLORI

The summit of artistry cannot be reached,

Nor does craftsman ever attain pure mastery.

Ptah-hotep

(*c.* 2350 B.C.)

CONTENTS

(An asterisk after a title indicates that the poem is accompanied by hieroglyphs.)

ILLUSTRATIONS

(Sources are listed on pages 117–118)

INTRODUCTION

THE love songs contained in this volume are almost all that remains to us, after the desiccations and tatters of three millennia, of what must have been an extensive body of secular lyric poetry written and sung in ancient Egypt. They are a precious inheritance; for as we read these poems, the dark of thirty centuries dissipates, and for a few moments we can feel— not merely intellectually consider, but *feel*—what it was like to live and be in love in the time of the last great pharaohs of Egypt. If, at least in our time, history seems to be one intolerable series of wars and rumors of war, songs like these prove that love also endures. And, indeed, the speakers in these poems, so long dead yet perennially young, show us that the varieties and moods of love then and in that civilization do not differ from our own. Their songs are romantic, idyllic, humorous, even satirical, sometimes naive, almost always graceful; and the singers self-sacrificing in the service of love, pure of heart, hesitant or intensely passionate, patently physical in their desire, or given to lust, sexual innuendo, and bawdry. Pretty much all the variations on the theme of love are there. The situations too are perennial: a lover describing his beloved, cataloguing all her beauties head to toe; a young girl out walking at night and (just accidentally, of course) passing by her boy friend's house; a couple sitting in the twilight after a hot day to catch the evening breeze in the garden; a girl coaxing her friend to go bathing with her by promising to wear her new swimsuit; a young sophisticate kneeling for an ironic prayer to Hathor, goddess of love, to retrieve his wandering girl friend. And so on.

The songs flash with a kaleidoscope of flowers, birds, gardens and orchards (trees were not so common in a narrow land flanked by twin deserts), irrigation canals, and always, the River. Yet the final effect, however idyllic, is not at all rural. It is more like pastoral, perhaps the first instances of the long pastoral tradition in literature, with, instead of shepherds, milkmaids, and flocks, a panorama of fowlers, birdcatchers' daughters, and hunting in the marsh. Indeed, these songs seem, by all the evidence we have, to be highly sophisticated compositions, written by poets, their names unknown after the lapse of time, who were very conscious of their craft and created the first examples of another long literary tradition—that of courtly love. Though individual lovers might be presented as naive, their creators certainly were not.

In fact, these love songs are the verbal equivalent of the lush, crowded, colorful scenes which have survived on the walls of ancient tombs in the City of the Dead at Thebes. Many of these and other tomb paintings were copied in tempera by Nina M. Davies during the early 1930s and thus—since ancient paintings fade and flake, and walls crumble —preserved for posterity. Those in this book are reproduced from photographs of the plates of Mrs. Davies' publication. Like the entertainments depicted there—the very noble ladies in their finest clothes and jewelry, the riot of foods and drinks, the naked servant girls, the singers, musicians, and dancers, and the harpists (often, like Homer, blind) plucking out dinner music—the love songs are full of life. And they similarly attest that these people of antiquity, far from being in love with death, as misinformation has it, were so delighted with life in the Nile Valley that they took great pains to preserve their bodies, which had served them so well in this world, in order to use them with equal happiness for eternity. In the love songs, the texture of this life has been caught forever.

The daily life—personal, unofficial, secular—which the songs preserve dates from the New Kingdom of pharaonic Egypt (c. 1600–1085 B.C.) and the last great flourishing of ancient Egyptian civilization. Indeed, the surviving copies of these poems were written down during the later New Kingdom, the time of the Ramesside pharaohs, and perhaps, as seen from a modern perspective, at a time when the long decline had already begun. For by 1000 B.C. the spirit of the place had departed.

Four small collections of poems have survived, three on papyri (Chester Beatty I and Harris 500 in the British Museum and Turin 1966 in the Egyptian Museum of Turin, Italy) and one on an ostracon (a piece of pottery or stone smoothed and used as a writing surface). This ostracon, number 25218 in the Cairo Museum in Egypt, consists of portions of a broken vase discovered in the nineteenth century. During the 1950s, French Egyptologists excavating a giant trash pit at the ancient workmen's village of Deir el Medineh in western Thebes discovered, among thousands of other ostraca, several more pieces of that same vase. These pieces were identified by Professor Georges Posener, working at the French Institute in Cairo; they were first published in 1972 as Ostracon Deir el Medineh 1266. The new pieces, joined with the fragments of the vase previously discovered, almost double the size of this fourth collection of love songs.

Scholars date these texts to Dynasties XIX and XX of the New Kingdom, or between 1300 and 1100 B.C.—about half a millennium before Homer. They were handwritten, in hieratic, the cursive form of the ancient hieroglyphic writing adapted to the use of brush and ink on papyrus or stone. I have translated them from photofacsimiles of the original texts published in scholarly editions. For a number of the poems I have drawn hieroglyphic transcriptions, which are printed alongside my English translations. Such transcriptions are normally made by Egyptologists when translating from the hieratic; mine depart from the usual practice only by being rearranged into the format of verse.

The individual lines of the ancient poem were sometimes, though not always, separated by means of dots, called "verse points," drawn in red ink as opposed to the black of the text. The poems themselves were separated, either by a brief notation at the beginning (often merely a number) to indicate the place of the poem in the total sequence—as in Papyrus Chester Beatty I—or by a sign (forearm with hand, palm down) at the close of the poem—as in Papyrus Harris 500. Some of the cycles had brief introductions, called "rubrics" because they were also drawn in red. Wherever verse points or rubrics occur, I have made use of them in my hieroglyphic transcriptions. The individual poems are not numbered here, but the poems within each song cycle appear in their original order. Not all of the cycles of poems have titles—in some cases they are simply lost. Where they survive, I have used them for the corresponding sections of this book; where they are missing I have supplied a descriptive title. Finally, the ancient scribe, to attest that he had been a faithful and accurate copyist, would often add a colophon to that effect at the end of his text. I too have followed the ancient practice.

In the several years I have spent translating these songs, I have tried never to forget that it was not a printing press or a photoduplicating machine but the living hand of some now forgotten Egyptian that once carefully—or sometimes not so carefully—formed the hieratic characters on a clean, untattered papyrus or an unchipped, unflaked ostracon. The owner of that hand was probably not the author of the song, and he may have been only a scribe copying out the text for his master, but someone thought enough of these lyrics to have them written down for his own library. For himself, not for us; but we have them, and they are ours now too.

If some Egyptian then could be moved and delighted by these songs, the modern translator, keeping faith with that dead hand from the past, must honor them as poems, making them new for his own time. From the beginning I have tried to follow two basic criteria: these ancient verses must sing as poetry to our modern ear, and they must be as faithful as knowledge of the ancient Egyptian language allows to the texture and idiom—the feel—of the original. We want to know the exact words of these speakers; but we also want to know the implications of their words, how they felt—about to love, in love, or the far side of love. The speakers must come alive again for us, after their millennia of frozen silence in the limbo of a lost language. Only in this way, in this kind of translation, can the continuity of human imagination and feeling over the centuries be perceived.

Some of the translations in this volume follow rather closely the original denotation of the words, the syntax, and the line arrangement—usually where the meaning, tone, and swing of the poem are clear in the original. In other cases, where meaning and tone, mood and feeling, are less clear, and connotations lost or all but inscrutable, I have dealt with the literal text with varying degrees of freedom. While little is known of the art of poetry in ancient Egypt, my study of the texts has suggested a kind of parallel in the language used by those American poets (Ezra Pound, William Carlos Williams, e. e. cummings, and others) prominent in the earlier decades of the twentieth century and writing in the "modernist" style. This prompted me to certain technical decisions: The translations should use the cadenced line, rhythmic, not metered; unrhymed; with verses of unequal length and following the phrasing and the prose accents of the speaking voice—for that seems best to capture the feel of the ancient line. The diction should be unpretentiously colloquial, simple, except when elevated by the power of strong feeling or slipping over into the sometimes slangy verbal patterns of irony or humor. The language should be conversational, quiet, the usages of personal and private speech; for those are the kinds of words for lovers. And the poems should be as full of imagery as the text allows—though this is no great problem, since the image system of a poem in an alien language translates most easily of all once one catches the implications conveyed by the image.

In many cases where words or phrases, and sometimes entire lines, of a poem are lacking, through a lacuna in the text, I have unashamedly supplied them as best I could, using as a more fundamental criterion respect for the integrity of the poem as a whole. Where too much of the piece was missing to recover a poem, I have not translated it. There are only a few such pieces; they occur primarily on scattered bits of ostraca apart from the collections mentioned, and at the end of Ostracon Deir el Medineh 1266. Since not enough of their spirit survives, I have, regretfully, omitted them.

But enough survives for us to be grateful. And I hope that in my versions these love songs wear the mantle of scholarship lightly, re-creating, for him who will read, people of flesh and blood out of the distant past.

❦ ONE ❧

Some Rather Lively Lines

(Papyrus Chester Beatty I: Recto)

Here begin some rather lively lines,

found in a book of writings, copied

by Nakht-Sobek, scribe

in the City of the Dead

A nobleman in the cool of his garden

Aim him straight at the house of your reticent lady

Aim him straight at the house of your reticent lady;
        storm, full cargo and sail, her true love's nest.
(Oh, throw the temple gates of her wide,
        his mistress readies for sacrifice!)

Fill her, with singing, with hurrying dances,
        wines, strong ale . . . (her Western places!) . . .
Waylay propriety. Then pay reward:
        finish her off in the night!

Thus will you hear her hushed saying,
        "Have me . . . close in your arms.
Even when dawn breaks in on tomorrow,
        let us be this way still."

Send him back hard by your lady's small window

Send him back hard by your lady's small window
                    (she is alone now, there is no other);
Stuff yourself full in her banquet hall!
                    Then through bedrock be shaken sky high,
Though very heaven break down in the stormwind,
                    he shall not (lovely lady) be moved.

Lo where she comes to you, bright with her thousand pleasures!
                    Fragrance spreads like a floodtide
Drowning the eyes, and the head whirls.
                    Unable the poor fool before her.

Ah! this is the hand of Our Golden Lady!—
                    She gives the girl as your due
That you keep to your service in Her Holy Name,
                    able anon, old pecker, to say
You've had the world in your time.

6

How clever my love with a lasso

How clever my love with a lasso—
                  she'll never need a kept bull!
She lets fly the rope at me
                  (from her dark hair),
Draws me in with her comehither eyes,
                  wrestles me down between her bent thighs,
Branding me hers with her burning seal.
                  (Cowgirl, the fire from those thighs!)

Why, just now, must you question your heart

Why, just now, must you question your heart?
> Is it really the time for discussion?
To her, say I,
> take her tight in your arms!
For god's sake, sweet man,
> it's me coming at you,
My tunic
> loose at the shoulder!

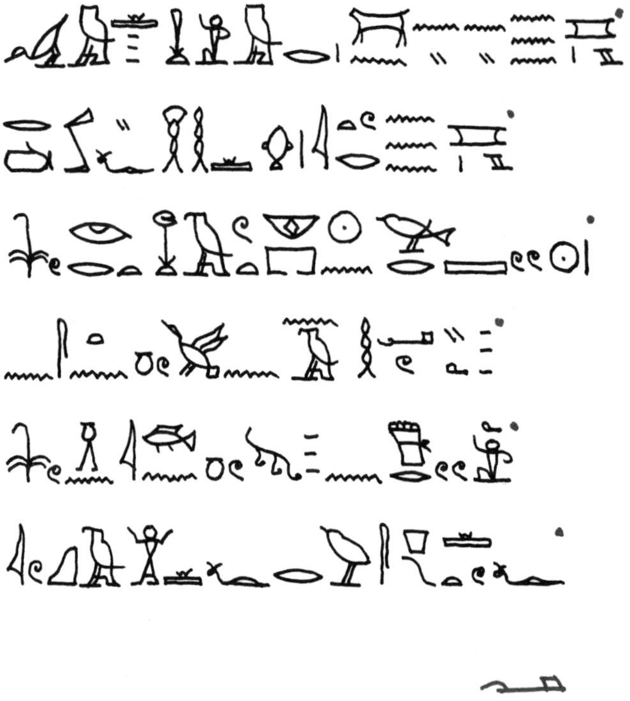

I found my love by the secret canal

I found my love by the secret canal,

                              feet dangling down in the water.

He had made a hushed cell in the thicket, for worship,

                              to dedicate this day

To holy elevation of the flesh.

He brings to light what is hidden

                              (breast and thigh go bare, go bare),

Now, raised on high toward his altar, exalted,

                              Ah! . . .

A tall man is more than his shoulders!

Ho, what she's done to me—that girl

Ho, what she's done to me—that girl!
               And I'm to grin and just bear it?
Letting me stand there huge in her door
               while she goes catfoot inside.
Not even a word: "Have a quiet walk home!"
               (dear god give me relief)
Stopping her ears the whole damned night
               and me only whispering, "Sharc!"

Once more you pass her house, deep in thought

Once more you pass her house, deep in thought,
               darkness is fallen, hiding you:

I would gain entry there,
               but for me no sort of welcome opens;
Yet the night is lovely for our soft purposes,
               and doors are meant to give passage!

Doorlatch, my friend, you govern my destiny:
               heaven for me needs a good turn from you;
(And once safe inside, our longhorn as payment)—
               oppose no spellbinding power!

Add oxen in praise to the door, as needed,
               lesser beasts to the lock, slit geese
To doorjamb and lintel, suet for sockets—
               and let all that moves turn quietly, quietly!

But the choicest cuts of our fine animal—
               these go instead to the sawyer's apprentice
If he makes us a new door—of rushes,
               and a tie-latch of brittlest straw.

O then, a man big with love could come anytime,
               find her house welcoming, open,

Discover the couch decked with closewoven bedclothes,

        and a lovely young lady restless among them!—

(You walk back and forth in the dark)

        She whispers:

"The mistress of this choice spot has been lonely.

        Dear heart, who held you so long?"

❧ TWO ❧

*Songs Inscribed
on an Earthen Vessel*

(Cairo Ostracon 25218, Augmented by Ostracon Deir El Medineh 1266)

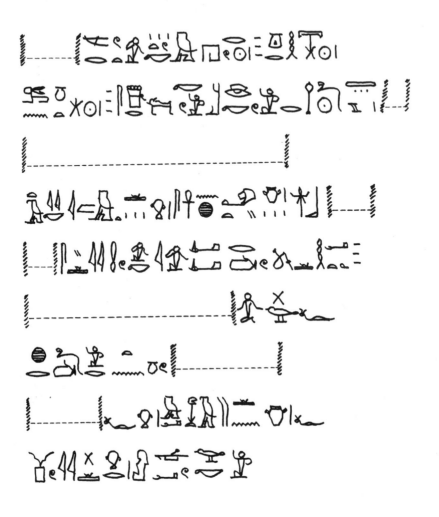

I love you through the daytimes

I love you through the daytimes,

　　　　　　　　　　　in the dark,

Through all the long divisions of the night,

　　　　　　　　　those hours

I, spendthrift, waste away alone,

　　　　　　　　　　and lie, and turn, awake till whitened dawn.

And with the shape of you I people night,

　　　　　　　　　　and thoughts of hot desire grow live within me.

What magic was it in that voice of yours

　　　　　　　　　to bring such singing vigor to my flesh,

To limbs which now lie listless on my bed without you?

Thus I beseech the darkness:

　　　　　　　　　Where gone, O loving man?

Why gone from her whose love

　　　　　　　　can pace you, step by step, to your desire?

　　　　　　　No loving voice replies.

And I (too well) perceive

　　　　　　　how much I am alone.

Your love, dear man, is as lovely to me

Your love, dear man, is as lovely to me
As sweet soothing oil to the limbs of the restless,

as clean ritual robes to the flesh of gods,
As fragrance of incense to one coming home

hot from the smells of the street.

It is like nipple-berries ripe in the hand,

like the tang of grainmeal mingled with beer,
Like wine to the palate when taken with white bread.

While unhurried days come and go,
Let us turn to each other in quiet affection,

walk in peace to the edge of old age.
And I shall be with you each unhurried day,

a woman given her one wish: to see
For a lifetime the face of her lord.

Love, how I'd love to slip down to the pond

Love, how I'd love to slip down to the pond,

                bathe with you close by on the bank.

Just for you I'd wear my new Memphis swimsuit,

                made of sheer linen, fit for a queen—

Come see how it looks in the water!

Couldn't I coax you to wade in with me?

                Let the cool creep slowly around us?

Then I'd dive deep down

                and come up for you dripping,

Let you fill your eyes

                with the little red fish that I'd catch.

And I'd say, standing there tall in the shallows:

Look at my fish, love,

                how it lies in my hand,

How my fingers caress it,

                slip down its sides . . .

But then I'd say softer,

                eyes bright with your seeing:

                        A gift, love. No words.

                Come closer and

                      look, it's all me.

I love a girl, but she lives over there

I love a girl, but she lives over there
                on the too far side of the River.
A whole Nile at floodstage rages between,
                and a crocodile hunched on the sand
Keeps motionless guard at the crossing.
                Still I go down to the water,
Stride out into the waves—
                how is it
Desire can soar in the wrench of this current,
                rough water be tame as my fields?
Why she loves me!   she loves me!   hers is the love
                anchors the shifting toeholds;
My charming girl whispered water magic
                (crocodile sits spellbound)—   O my love,
Where are you, whose hand
                is so small yet has mastered the River?
—There, over there! already waiting,
                right in the path of my burning eyes!
The only one dear to my heart,
                and she crowns the shore like a queen!

My love is back, let me shout out the news

My love is back, let me shout out the news!
　　　　　My arms swing wide to embrace her,
And heart pirouettes in its dark chamber
　　　　　glad as a fish when night shades the pool.
You are mine, my mistress, mine to eternity,
　　　　　mine from the day you first whispered my name!

Singers and dancers

When I hold my love close

When I hold my love close

               (and her arms steal around me),
I'm like a man translated to Punt

               or like someone out in the reedflats
When the whole world suddenly bursts into flower.

               In this dreamland of South Sea fragrances,
My love, you are essence of roses.

When we kiss, and her warm lips half open

When we kiss, and her warm lips half open,

               I fly cloud-high without beer!

What paradise gained, what fulfillment,

               what a heavenly turn of affairs!

Oh, raise one to Menkat, Our Lady of Liquor,

               but keep your mouth tight on the girl!

If now, my little maid, you are quite finished

If now, my little maid, you are quite finished

        trotting to and fro to dress milady's chamber

(My dear opponent waiting now therein),

        I thus instruct you:

Arrange your whitest sheets about her dusky body

        (above   below   behind   between)

—For her no bedtime in mere royal linen,

        and girl, beware coarse common cloth—

Then grace her in her sheerest tunic,

        touch her with your rarest perfumes,

And go.

        She is prepared.

I wish I were her Nubian girl

I wish I were her Nubian girl,

           one to attend her (bosom companion),

Confidante, and a child of discretion:

           Close hidden at nightfall we whisper

As (modest by day) she offers

           breasts like ripe berries to evening—

Her long gown settles, then, bodiless,

           hangs from my helping hand.

Oh, she'll give pleasure!   In future

           no grown man will deny it!

But tonight, to me, this chaste girl

           bares unthinking the delicate blush

Of a most secret landscape,

           her woman's body.

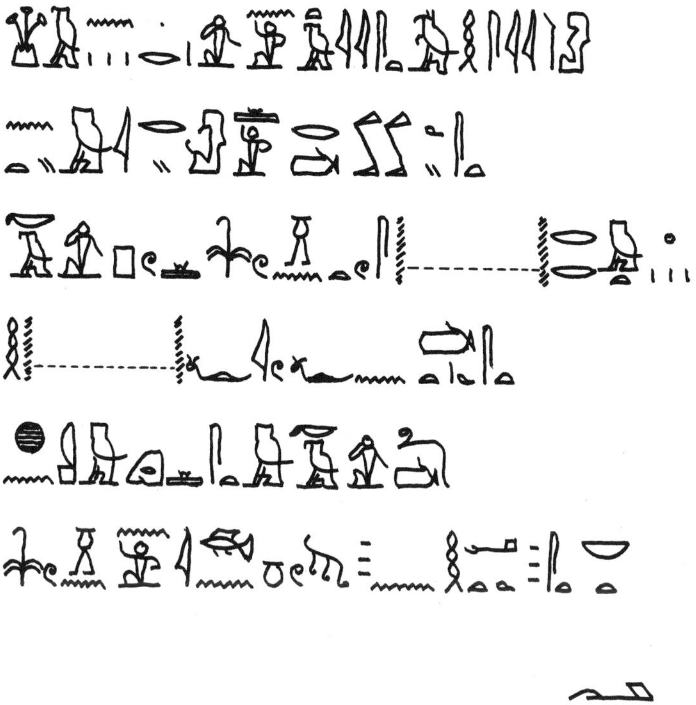

If I could just be the washerman

If I could just be the washerman

              doing her laundry for one month only,

I would be faithful to pick up the bundles,

              sturdy to beat clean the heavy linens,

But gentle to touch those finespun things

              lying closest the body I love.

I would rinse with pure water the perfumes

              that linger still in her tunics,

And I'd dry my own flesh with the towels

              she yesterday held to her face.

The touch of her clothes, their textures,

              her softness in them . . .

Thank god for the body,

              its youthful vigor!

❧ THREE ❧

Songs of the Garden

(Papyrus Harris 500: Song Cycle III)

Here begin songs of the heart's enjoying

A pool in a garden

My always love, believe

My always love, believe,

Desire is measured out to me as much as you;

so let me do, dear heart,

My heart's desire with you.

. . . And I am in your arms . . .

(But let me paint my eyes, I beg you,

to see you is a shining dazzles them,

And I crave shade and shadow).

I curl against you,

For I would know again the mastery

by which you prove

How well you love me

(past master of my heart),

Remembering that hour,

hushed and holy—

Out of eternity a moment streaked to mark me

the night I slept with you.

My eager heart leaps toward you now:

Yes!   I'm the one

For him I love

in the night that belongs to me!

Palm trees, heavy with dates

Palm trees, heavy with dates,

        bend over my private garden;

Among such towering friends

        grow tall toward your private dream.

Dear heart, it is I am your chiefest love,

        first bud from the ground of your caring,

And I give back that love, am yours—

        take me and my gift of a garden.

I planted it, weeded it, loved it,

        nursed it to bear this thicket of colors,

Heady with foreign blossoms,

        heavy with all sweet native flowers.

A fountain plays in my garden,

        bubbles below the tall sun,

For dipping your hand in

        while easy we lie

Waiting the cool of the northern seabreeze

        that springs upriver at twilight.

A charming spot to stroll,

        your hand covering mine;

My body enjoys, relaxes, plays . . .

        Oh, how my heart is high

Matching the swing of our going—together,

        halves of a single love!

The sound of your voice is sweet,

        full like the taste of date wine,

And I, drunken girl in a tangle of flowers,

        live only, a captive, to hear it.

But to have you here always, tall in my garden,

        devour you with my hungry eyes—

Love, I'd be raised to pure spirit, translated,

        hovering high over earth!

(See me go!   light-hearted!   walking on air!)

        Full of such love,

I scorn, insubstantial, the grossness of eating,

        drinking, light-headed, the bright date wine.

I strip you of your tangled garlands

I strip you of your tangled garlands,

Once you are back again, O drunken man

sprawled deep in sleep (and gone) in bed.

I stroke your feet

while children . . . . . .

[*Here the papyrus begins to tatter.*]

. . . cry out wild with longing . . . .

[*The rest is lost.*]

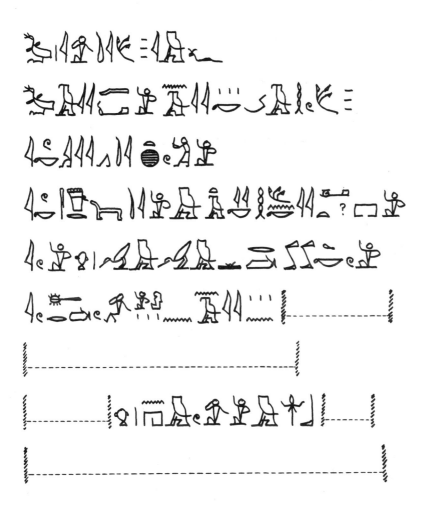

❧ FOUR ❧

Songs of Great Heart's Ease

(Papyrus Chester Beatty I: Verso)

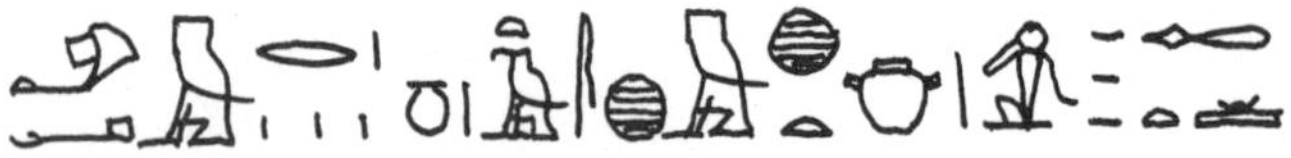

Beginning of the songs

of

great heart's ease

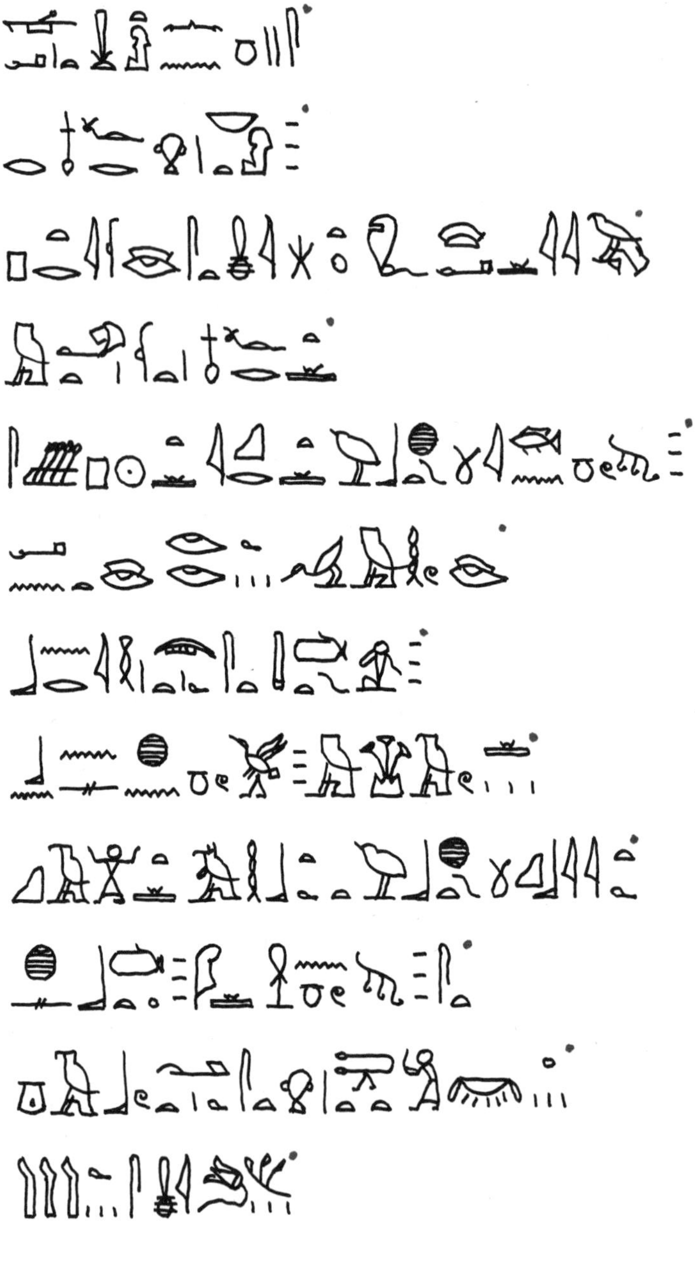

My love is one and only, without peer

My love is one and only, without peer,

        lovely above all Egypt's lovely girls.

On the horizon of my seeing,

        see her, rising,

Glistening goddess of the sunrise star

        bright in the forehead of a lucky year.

So there she stands, epitome

        of shining, shedding light,

Her eyebrows, gleaming darkly, marking

        eyes which dance and wander.

Sweet are those lips, which chatter

        (but never a word too much),

And the line of the long neck lovely, dropping

        (since song's notes slide that way)

To young breasts firm in the bouncing light

        which shimmers that blueshadowed sidefall of hair.

And slim are those arms, overtoned with gold,

        those fingers which touch like a brush of lotus.

And (ah) how the curve of her back slips gently

        by a whisper of waist to god's plenty below.

(Such thighs as hers pass knowledge

        of loveliness known in the old days.)

Dressed in the perfect flesh of woman

        (heart would run captive to such slim arms),

      she ladies it over the earth,

Schooling the neck of each schoolboy male

        to swing on a swivel to see her move.

(He who could hold that body tight

          would know at last

              perfection of delight—

Best of the bullyboys,

       first among lovers.)

Look you, all men, at that golden going,

        like Our Lady of Love,

             without peer.

My love's a mischiefmaker

My love's a mischiefmaker—

         voice that heats my heart

While he stands by to let lovelonging

         play riot on my body.

He lives just down the street . . . so near . . .

         settler among Mother's people,

But I don't dare go out to see him . . .

(I wonder, could Mother be good at such things?

         Lady of Love, send her light!)

My heart beats hard, remembering him,

         love rides off with me captive.

What a fool of a mad boy he is!

         (but then, I'm everyway like him)

And he can't even know I am crazy to touch him

         (please, write just a nice note to Mother!)

Love, O my love, I'll be yours—

         One Golden of Women commands it.

Come to me, meet me, come

         let me feel how handsome you are . . .

How happy Father and Mother would be!

Why, the whole street together would turn out to shout,

         sing and chant, carry on in your honor!

My people would welcome you one of our own—

         how I will make them dance for you, love!

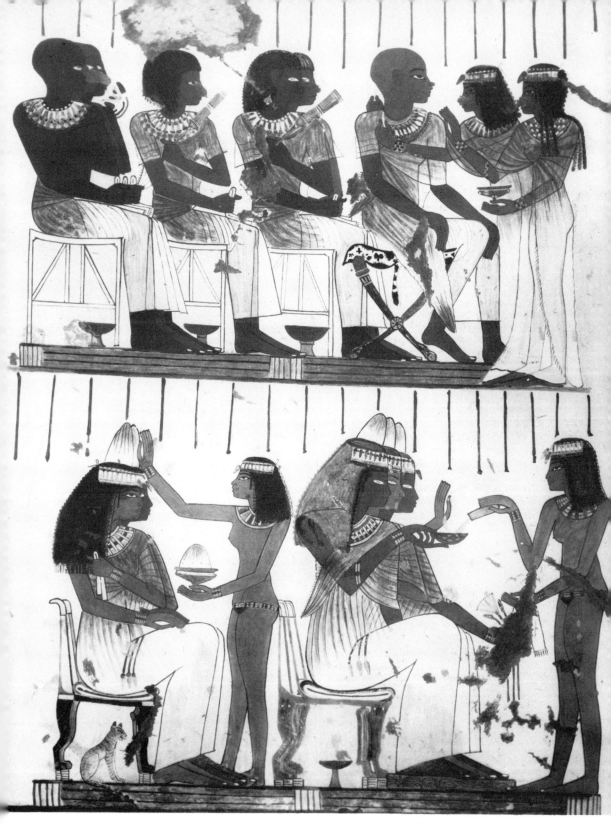

Guests at a feast

I was simply off to see Nefrus my friend

I was simply off to see Nefrus my friend,
Just to sit and chat at her place

                     (about men),

When there, hot on his horses, comes Mehy

          (Oh god, I said to myself, it's Mehy!)

Right over the crest of the road

                 wheeling along with the boys.

O Mother Hathor, what shall I do?

          Don't let him see me!

                 Where can I hide?

Make me a small creeping thing

          to slip by his eye

               (sharp as Horus')

                        unseen.

Oh, look at you, feet—

          (this road is a river!)

               you walk me right out of my depth!

Someone, silly heart, is exceedingly ignorant here—

          aren't you a little too easy near Mehy?

If he sees that I see him, I know

          he will know how my heart flutters (Oh,

                      Mehy!).

I know I will blurt out,

"Please take me!"

(I mustn't)

No, all he would do is brag out my name,

just one of the many . . . (I know) . . .

Mehy would make me just one of the girls

for all of the boys in the palace

(oh Mehy).

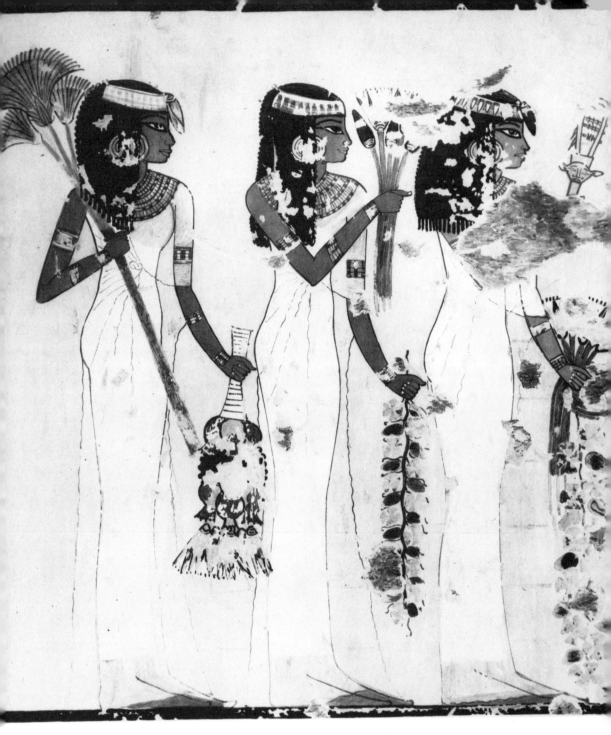

Girls bringing fruit and flowers

Flee him, my heart—and hurry

Flee him, my heart—and hurry!—

        for I know all too well this love of yours.
—My antic heart won't let me walk like others

        but dances off just when I want it home.
It will not wait to let me catch my tunic

        nor stop to let me get my party fan;
It leaves no time to shadow eyes with love lines,

        no time at all to oil my unloved body.

"Don't stand there waiting! Get inside!"

        so heart says as I stand there full of him.
O heart, don't make my aching thoughts turn foolish!

        Why, are we mad? who gave you leave?

                (It's wrong!)

Sit cool, my love, your love comes soon to you.

        But no . . . no, after all . . . there are so many eyes!
These people must not mock me, hissing,

        "You, sister! It's love gone tripping made you fall!"
Hold firm your ground, girl, when you long for him;

        and heart, you shall not flee.

Now I shall kneel, praising the Golden Girl

Now I shall kneel, praising the Golden Girl,
For I (unaccountably) find myself absent,
                    out of Her circle of love.
Let me forthwith extol the great Queen of Heaven
                    (butter up Hathor: Lady, I love you),
Perform proper thanksgiving for Our Madam's favors,
Then (with suitable diffidence) push my complaint
                    that She hear my petition—now!
"Lady, give me that girl for my own,
                    set her aside for just me!"

But wait—O my goddess—she's here,
                    returned on her own to my eyes!
(What a happening this is)
                    "It's her in the flesh!"
I rejoice;   I am glad;
                    I'm enlarged with delight!
And just look at those musclemen congregate,
                    bowing and scraping,
Flexing their biceps,
                    bulging with love of her!

            . . . well, so dreams fade . . .

54

Now I must bow to my Goddess—again—

        heave breath for another prayer:

"Lady, give me something sufficient for sickness,

        give me my love as a remedy!"

It's five days now since I first prayed her name.

Lady, here I kneel sickening—

        where the hell is she?

I just chanced to be happening by

I just chanced to be happening by
                in the neighborhood where he lives;
His door, as I hoped, was open—
                and I spied on my secret love.
How tall he stood by his mother,
                brothers and sisters little about him;
Love steals the heart of a poor thing like me
                pointing her toes down his street.
And how gentle my young love looked
                (there's none like him),
Character spotless they say . . .
                out of the edge of my eye
I caught him look at me as I passed.

Alone by myself at last,
                I could almost cry with delight!
Now, just a word with you, love,
                that's what I've wanted since I first saw you.
If only Mother knew of my longing
                (and let it occur to her soon)—
O Golden Lady, descend for me,
                plant him square in her heart!

Then I'd run to my love, kiss him hard

               right in front of his crew.

I'd drip no tears of shame or shyness

               just because people were there,

But proud I'd be at their taking it in

               (let them drown their eyes in my loving you)

If you only acknowledge you know me.

               (Oh, tell all Egypt you love me!)

Then I'd make solemn announcement:

               every day holy to Hathor!

And we two, love, would worship together,

               kneel, a matched pair, to the Goddess.

Oh, how my heart pounds (try to be circumspect!)

               eager to get myself out!

Let me drink in the shape of my love

               tall in the shuddering night!

Last night made it seven my eyes missed my kitten

Last night made it seven my eyes missed my kitten—
>   I'm a tottering outpost invaded by sickness,
Love-lethargy leaves my limbs logy,
>   I stagger about with a low-grade fever,
Sometimes I drift into reverie . . .
>   sometimes don't even remember my name . . .

Let them call in the whole crew of specialists,
>   my heart will not tick to their remedies,
Or let reader-priests come mumbling their gibberish—
>   all their spells and charms, a dead end too.
Not one can finger the source of my symptoms!—
>   (she's the soft devil who drugged me).

But if someone would say, "There's a lady here, waiting"—
>   hear that, and you'd see me take heart in a hurry!
>   (her name would perk up my members)—
Or only her messengers coming and going:
>   their running would quicken my pulse!

Why, that girl's better than any prescription,
>   more to me than the Pharmacopoeia—
My own secret Hathor Home Remedy?—
>   Her slipping into my room from the road!
>   (have *her* examine me, *then* watch my energy!)

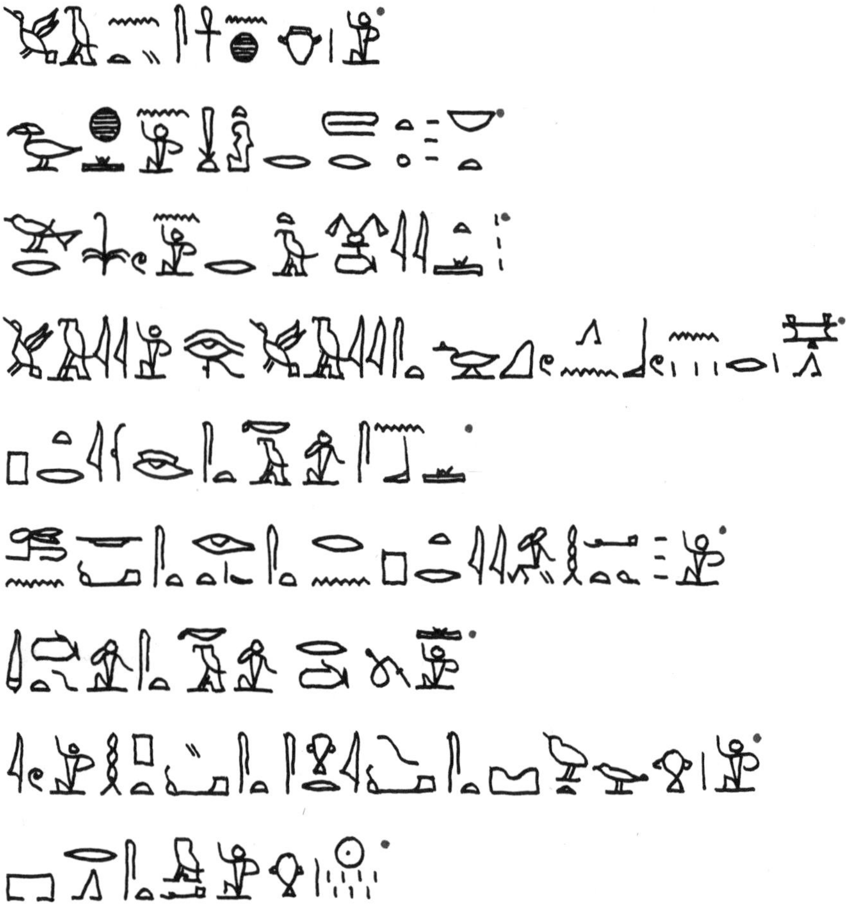

And just let her look me full in the eye,

       every bit of my body is back in its prime.

At the sound of her voice my heart leaps to her tune,

And then when I kiss her, feel her length breast to thigh,

       Love's evil spirits fly clean from my system—

          God, what a girl, what a woman! . . .

And that bitch has been gone for a week!

❧ FIVE ❧

Songs from a Faded Papyrus

(Papyrus Harris 500: Song Cycle I)

Birds in an acacia tree

If ever, my dear one, I should not be here

If ever, my dear one, I should not be here,

                where will you offer your heart?

If I cannot hold you close by my side,

                how will you ever know love's satisfaction?

Would your fingers follow the line of my thighs,

                learn the curve of my breasts, and the rest?

It is all here, love,

                quickly uncovered.

Yet would you leave me now

                out of some urge that mankind must eat?

By god is your only organ your belly?

                —are you in love with digestion?

Or is it a matter of dress makes you restless?

                (would you feel naked above me?)

I'm a woman of means—I'll lend you bedclothes!

                What is this hunger

Pricks you to go from me? . . . what can I say? . . .

                Here, hold my breasts to you—

Yours, my offering, full like the love I give

                overflowing, unending . . . (untold) . . .

How splendid a whole day made holy by loving

                    (being in touch face to face)—

More than a million times over, my couchmate,

              it shall be heaven,

                            good for the soul!

Love of you is mixed deep in my vitals

Love of you is mixed deep in my vitals,

            like water stirred into flour for bread,

Like simples compound in a sweet-tasting drug,

            like pastry and honey mixed to perfection.

Oh, hurry to look at your love!

            Be like horses charging in battle,

Like a gardener up with the sun

            burning to watch his prize bud open.

High heaven causes a girl's lovelonging.

            It is like being too far from the light,

Far from the hearth of familiar arms.

            It is this being so tangled in you.

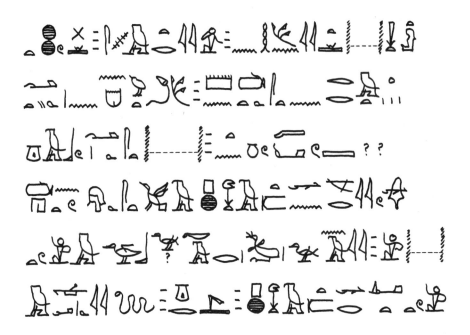

Astray or captured, all bear witness

Astray or captured, all bear witness

        to the consummate skill of this lady,
Shrewd at her craft and perfected by heaven.

        Her hand has the feel of new-blown lotus,
Her breast the delicate scent of ripe berries,

        her arms twine like vinestems, and tangle,
And her face is a snare of fine-grained redwood.

        And I?   who am I in this recital?—
The proverbial goose

        (and my love it is lures me)
Tricked by her tasty bait

        to this trap of my own ingenious imagining.

I cannot condone, my heart, your loving

I cannot condone, my heart, your loving

        this son of a wild dog who mounted you drunk;

Yet I'll never leave him to judgment, and beating,

        or wear out my day in recrimination.

Shall I (as they tell me) club him to Syria,

        cudgel the cur to Nubian exile?

Harry him to the highlands high over me,

        batter him down to the river mud?

No, not an ear for their harsh clamor!

        I'll never forswear our swift-running love!

Oh, I'm bound downstream on the Memphis ferry

Oh, I'm bound downstream on the Memphis ferry,

                like a runaway, snapping all ties,

With my bundle of old clothes over my shoulder.

I'm going down there where the living is,

                going down there to that big city,

And there I'll tell Ptah (Lord who loves justice):

                "Give me a girl tonight!"

Look at the River!   eddying,

                in love with the young vegetation.

Ptah himself is the life of those reedshoots,

                Lady Sakhmet of the lilies—

Yes, Our Lady of Dew dwells among lilypads—

                and their son, Nefertem, sweet boy,

Blossoms newborn in the blue lotus.

                Twilight is heavy with gods . . .

And the quiet joy of tomorrow,

                dawn whitening over her loveliness:

O Memphis my city, beauty forever!—

                you are a bowl of love's own berries,

Dish set for Ptah your god,

                god of the handsome face.

I think I'll go home and lie very still

I think I'll go home and lie very still,

                 feigning terminal illness.

Then the neighbors will all troop over to stare,

                 my love, perhaps, among them.

How she'll smile while the specialists

                 snarl in their teeth!—

                 she perfectly well knows what ails me.

So there's love's country nest

So there's love's country nest
                (a whole estate)!
The central gateway there . . .
                and there's her house . . .
Double door swung open,
                the half-seen inner chambers—
Well, out she'll be soon,
                furious I followed.

I wish I were doorman
                guarding that gateway!
I'd stop her passage,
                hold her for questioning
                (just a petty official doing his duty),
Then sit to enjoy the range of her voice
                as she raged like a fury on and on,
Child of her own imperious anger.

74

Craftsmen at work

I'm going downstream on Kingswater Canal

I'm going downstream on Kingswater Canal,

        with leave to attend Sun Festival;

I want to wander there where the tents

        are pitched at the far end of Mertiu Lagoon.

I'll hurry along—I can hardly keep silent—

        thinking of God's holy Day,

For maybe I'll see my truelove go by

        bound for the Houses of Offering.

I'll stand there with you at the mouth of the Mertiu

        (heart, are you with me or back in Rē's city?),

Then we'll turn back to Offeringhouse Orchard,

        where I'll steal from the grove by the chapels

A branch for a festival fan.

        There I can watch the whole celebration.

With my eyes upturned toward the holy garden,

        and my arms full of flowering branches,

And my hair heavy with sweetsmelling unguents,

        what a splendid Lady I'll be!—

Dressed fine like a princess, for Rē,

        Lord of Two Lands, on His feast day.

Fine like a bride, love,

        I'll stand there (waiting) beside you.

76

❦ SIX ❧

Stanzaic Love Song

(Papyrus Chester Beatty I: Verso)

Horses and mules at the harvest field

I

Oh, might I speed you on toward your love,

        quick, like a king's man commanded to hurry!

See how His Majesty's thoughts hang on the heels of his messenger,

        his heart all attention, eager for news.

Stable doors to land's end swing free to that envoy,

        fresh horses are his at each station,

And a chariot, harnessed, always stands ready to go—

        not for him to take ease on the way.

      But once he has reached the nest of his love,

        his mission accomplished,

      Let his heart there dally delighted.

II

Oh, might I welcome you

        as the King's own steed is welcome,

A champion chosen from thousands,

        thoroughbred, best in the stables.

He is one (my love) who has earned what is his,

        whose Master can trust his surefooted stepping.

And just let him hear the call of the whip,

        his high spirits know no delay;

Not even the best of the Syrian groomsmen

        stands in his path to head him off.

      How well the heart of a girl can feel it

        (charge on and on, my lovely stallion)

      When her love's not far away.

III

Oh, might I speed you on toward your love!

Be quick like the sleek gazelle

        bounding in flight down the paths of the desert.

Its hot hooves burn; its body grows weary;

        mortal terror stabs into its sides;

Hunters are after it,

        hounds all but up with it—

Then its dust disappears and it's gone . . . (dear beast) . . .

        pursuers no longer discern it;

For it found how reeds make for safety, a haven,

        how the riverbank route means escape.

        Love, may you likewise reach haven

                here in my she-lion's den

        (this huntress never would harm you);

        Just come to my cave's mouth,

                I'll take you in

        and cover your hands with my kisses.

You are doomed to track down my love

        until, by the Golden Goddess, I catch you.

Oh, may She make the fields of my longing

        spring green in the sun until harvest!

❧ SEVEN ❧

Songs of the Orchard

(Papyrus Turin 1966)

Men gathering figs

The pomegranate bush raises its voice

The pomegranate bush raises its voice
        (tiny, insistent, and shrill):
My seeds shine like the teeth of my mistress,
        the shape of my fruit is round like her breasts.
I'm her favorite, I know, sweetest tree in the orchard,
        looking my best through every season.

I gather my girl and her lover together;
        it's my arms they lie under on a limp day
Happy and high on wine and my cider,
        their bodies streaming with sweet-oil.

All other trees grow fainthearted, and droop;
        uncaring, they let their leaves die.
But I am busy twelve months of the year,
        fruitfullest of her small servants.
I stand with head high when a flower of mine falls:
        one left from last year curls inside me.

I live above that inconstant crew;
        yet, shaking their fingers, they whisper, "How little!"
Let it happen again (just once more!)
        and I break my decent silence about them.
One would like, of course, to be kind to one's neighbors,
        but their envy is patently obvious.

83

I must write out a lesson for my beloved:

"Do not, Madam, undervalue a friend."

Let my love love me best and I shall ordain

her hands full of lotus blossoms, and flowers,

Full of buds, and perfumes, strong ale,

and beer, why, of every brewable kind!

Then she'll give you, her love, a day to remember . . .

(the reed hut waits, the spot is secluded)

Oh, look!   (don't whisper)   he's really coming!

Let's all flatter him, girls, tell him he's handsome!

Make him drink down this day to its last shadow,

for our mistress, hidden,

by her slim side.

When the fig feels called to speak its mind

When the fig feels called to speak its mind,

        moving leaves begin to whisper:

If she ever decided to ask it,

        I would quietly die for my mistress.

        (Was ever lady so noble as Me?)

If ever her quickhanded slaves were not there,

        it is I would play humble servant.

I was brought from a wet, hostile land,

        uprooted as plunder for my beloved.

She had them set me here in the orchard;

        she saved me.

But the dear never lets me spend my day drinking

        nor fills my insides with sweet ditchwater.

How in the world can a girl enjoy life

        with such terrible thirst and not drinking?

By my deathless soul (if it survives),

        sweetheart, fetch me some water!

When her little sycamore, petite, begins to speak

When her little sycamore, petite, begins to speak

                    (uncommon among common trees),

The murmur of its leaves

                    (loquacious leaves, coquettish leaves,

                              its leaves of many voices)

Drips honey in the ear;

                  its fragrant words taste sweet.

Her own hand, soft as lotus, delicate,

          held it gently, planted it—

                      her favorite tree.

                      How lovely!

(And like its guardian goddess, full of love.)

What sheen of interwoven red and green!

Carved emerald is pale beside its branches,

                  boughs arching gracefully

                  (love renews endlessly);

Heavy with figs

        redder than jasper

                ready to fall

                (love is a harvest

                lover take all);

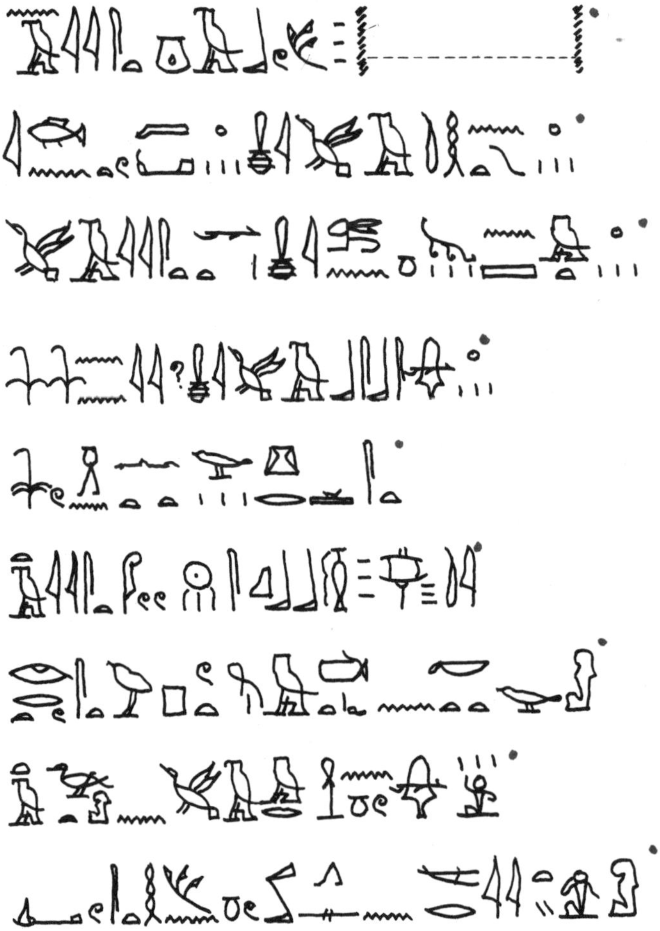

Malachite leaves,

        bark like green jasper

                (lady waits willingly

                must lover ask her?).

It lures those lounging in the garden;

        on lovers drawn light filters down;

            the Eye of Rē is hidden.

Garden freshens in its shadows;

           mellow the muted air.

It catches Great Green's gift of seabreeze;

        rustle covers private whispers;

              lovers linger.

For Hathor, Queen of Heaven,

        queen of love,

Queen of all little sycamores

        in love

     with mistresses who plant them

            out of love,

It spreads its balanced branches, full of love.

Its shadows deepen dark eyes

        dark with love.

II

The little sycamore (perfect tree) secretly

     slips a love-note to a certain girl—

Gardener's daughter, daughter of the garden

        (mistress of a certain tree)—

Commands her,

        sends her running to her love

                (quick feet, sandaled, skim the sand):

"Nehet here greets you:

        Come.

Pass a fleeting moment with my girls;

            cool an hour from sun in shadow.

It's garden's heyday; love runs green;

            private the arbor below.

The guests in my garden would welcome to see you;

            hearts would rejoice at your coming.

                    (Indeed!)

For your sake (and hers) send servants to stagger

            laden with banquet beneath me.

                Join the festivity!

(To run to you makes Someone

            drunk with no winecup spent!

Slim bearer of these words

            is innocent of their intent:

                Keep silent!)

      Hers,

        Nehet."

III

The servants have brought the provisions,

        pavilion bursts with the banquet;

Food overflows, and delight, and their laughter.

The flowers—lotus, papyrus,

Blossoms of garden, marshland, and village,

      flowers Rē opened at his last passing,

      flowers Rē shines on today,

        buds brought before their love ripened—

           all color the garden today.

Drink and song!

      And girls in their summer dresses!

Light hearts discover each other, seek cover,

          lady by lover.

Oh, Mother Hathor,

      hear your small sycamore!

Let her, my mistress,

      spend the day happily:

Not the hour of my letter,

Not the fleet moment,

      meeting and glancing,

But morning by noon

      and hushed dark after;

Day after day, the third day thereafter.

         Hear her heart sing?

         Hear her laughter?

Let her lie in my shade with her lover—

      my mistress, his lady.

So tall by her side: it is right, it is fitting.

She raises his cup to him,

                hangs on his words,

Bright in the service of love.

Around them, down byways of garden, air thickens;

                  guests grow drunken in whispers.

Song and strong drink:

                 light heads hang heavier,

                 paired heads go down.

But she keeps apart with her partner, discreetly,

                 walking beneath me,

                     in love as she goes.

    (She whispers;

             he looks at her;

                  smiling they go.)

    Mother Hathor,

         I know:

           I am a chatterer.

But my mistress, I love her!

             Her arms, they once held me!

Nehet will protect her:

           her secret is safe

           (all her words, all the rest),

Safe in a meaningless

          whisper of sycamore leaves,

Safe in the meaningless

          song of Nehet.

❦ EIGHT ❦

Songs of the Birdcatcher's Daughter

(Papyrus Harris 500: Song Cycle II)

Here begin songs to distract the heart. . . .

Imagine in this girl the charm of your own love,

dear to your heart,

as she comes to you from the meadow.

Fowling in the marshes

Lover, beloved, strongwinged love

Lover, beloved, strongwinged love,

          my heart like a huntress follows your flight.

A girl's sleepy feelings, wakened by you—

          you've made a whole world for me!

Here I am, breathless, fresh from my snares,

          birdgear still in my hands,

Throwstick and net . . . (I am ready) . . .

          For love of god, come a-hunting!

Why, every last singer from Punt's here in Egypt,

          flew down covered with myrrh to the ears!

The first one came, and he pounced on my baitworm

          (odor of spice hung thick on the breeze),

And his talons were sticky with sweetgum.

          My heart turns to you, begging,

Let's free him together, we two,

          out where I have you alone.

Let yourself go, hear the voice (how he cries!)

          of my hostage crestfallen with myrrh.

How good it would be, just you there with me,

          while I set my carefullest trap!

And what luck for a lover—outbound for the marsh

          with that special one waiting to love!

Voice of the wild goose crying

Voice of the wild goose crying,

                calling me, caught by my lure . . .

But your loving me slows my going,

                tangled, I cannot work free.

Love, let me go,

                nets of my own need untying!

And what am I going to tell Mother?

                Each day's end returning to her

Bent double under my catch . . .

                Haiee! no tripping the snarelines today!

Wild goose, I hear your call,

                I'm captive, taken by love of you!

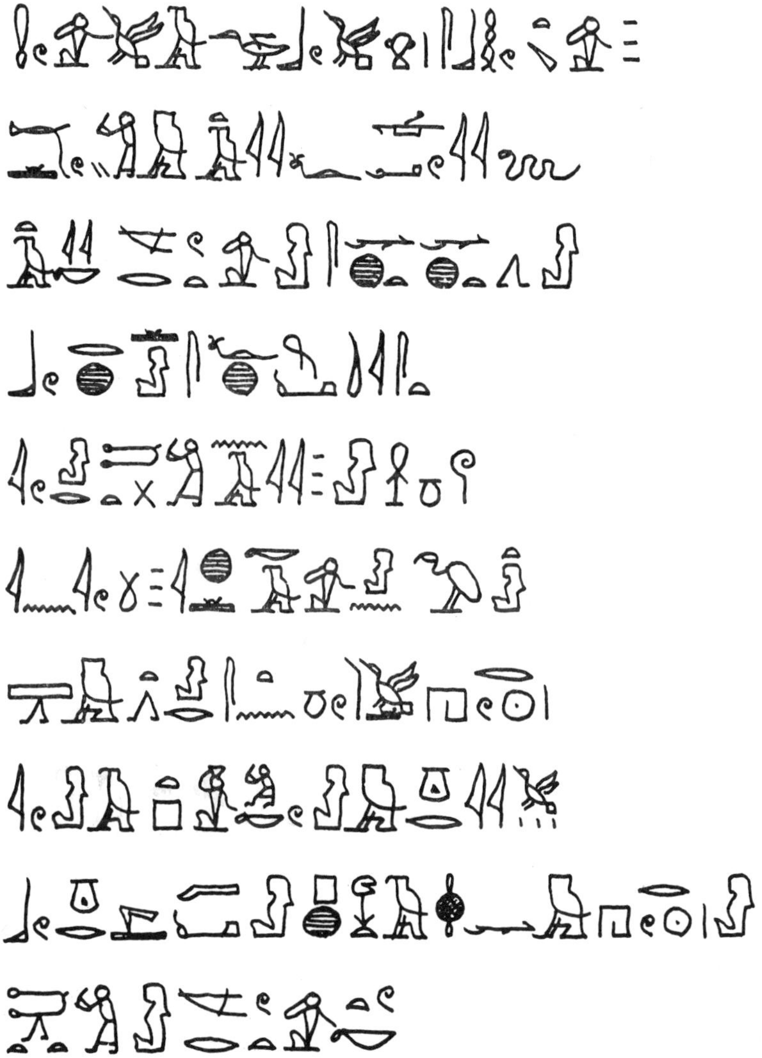

The wild goose bursts into flight, then settles

The wild goose bursts into flight, then settles
                beating his wings in distraction,
Mischiefmaker tearing the meshes,
                scourge of the birdcote.
Birds, thick as lizards, mill about squawking,
                and all is confusion.

I do not flutter, though caught
                (singing bird) in invisible net.
Lonely, I lift up my call
                under the weight of my love:

This heart is counterpoise to your own.
                I shall never be far.
Balance my love with your caring.

Whenever I leave you, I go out of breath

Whenever I leave you, I go out of breath

        (death must be lonely like I am);

I dream lying dreams of your love lost,

        and my heart stands still inside me.

I stare at my favorite datecakes—

        they would be salt to me now—

And pomegranate wine (once sweet to our lips)

        bitter, bitter as birdgall.

Touching noses with you, love, your kiss alone,

        and my stuttering heart speaks clear:

Breathe me more of your breath, let me live!

        Man meant for me,

God himself gave you as his holy gift,

        my love to outlast forever.

Officers of a noble household bringing offerings

What heaven it would be

What heaven it would be

    if my heart's own wish came true,
To care for all you have and are,

    housemistress of the manor!

While your arm lies gentle on my breast

    (which twists, unquiet, out of love),
I send my stealthy wish to creep inside you

    (praying, Deliver him to me!).
My love, oh, marry! be, in the darkness of this night,

    my lord, husband to me,
Or yet another girl walks lonely to her tomb.

    For who else gives good health and life?
Delight me with the air of your lifegiving,

    be prodigal,
Capitulate, let in

    this wandering heart which seeks you.

The voice of the swallow, flittering, calls to me

The voice of the swallow, flittering, calls to me:
        "Land's alight! Whither away?"
No, little bird, you cannot entice me,
        I follow you to the fields no more.

Like you in the dawn mist I rose,
        at sunrise discovered my lover abed
                (his voice is sweeter).
"Wake," I said, "or I fly with the swallow."
And my heart smiled back
        when he, smiling, said:
"You shall not fly,
        nor shall I, bright bird.
                But hand in hand
We shall walk the Nileside pathways,
        under cool of branches, hidden
                (only the swallows watching)—
Wide-eyed girl,
        I shall be with you in all glad places."

Can you match the notes of that song, little swallow?
        I am first in his field of girls!
My heart, dear sister, sings in his hand—
        love never harmed a winged creature.

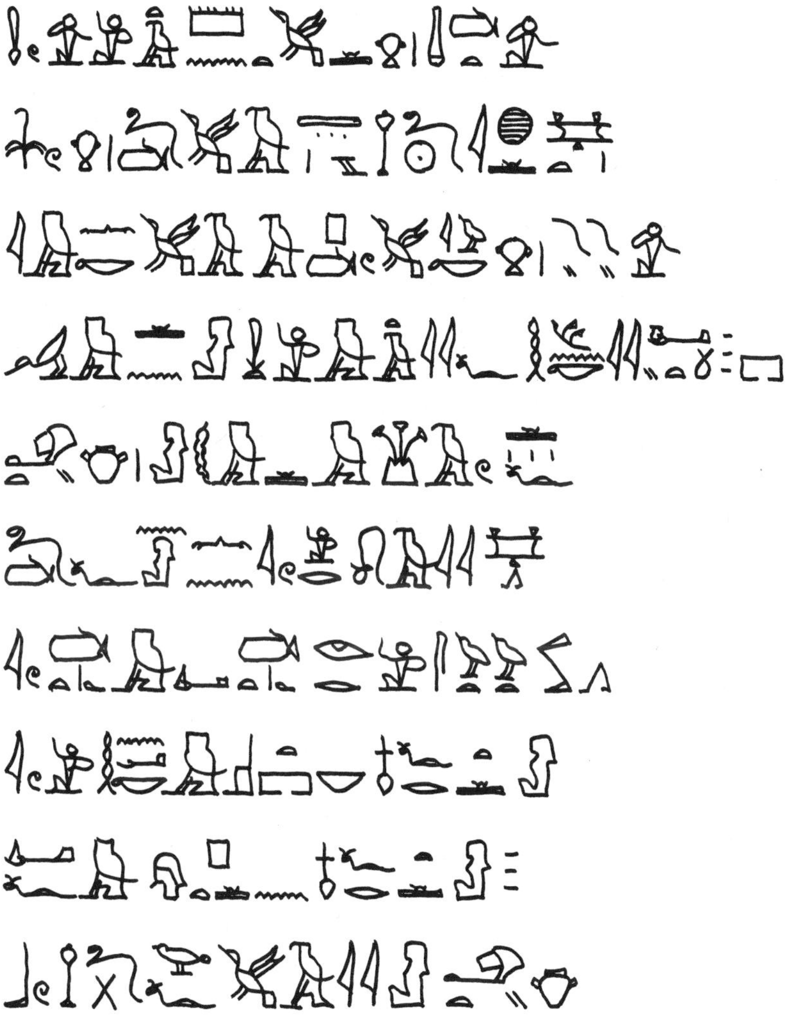

Let me look through his wayside gate

Let me look through his wayside gate—

        I think it's my love there, coming for me!

Eyes on the ground but my ears listening hard,

        I tremble a little, waiting for him.

(I'll make an art out of loving my love,

        he'll be my only concern!)

For him heart stops at nothing!

Why, he's sending me only a messenger!

        the one with fast slinky feet,

Trusted with bedroom secrets

        . . . (I never liked him) . . .

A mere servant tells me my love's been a lie!

        "He's found another."

Whose turn is it now

        making soft eyes up into his face . . . ?

            . . . oh my god, love,

What kind of man breaks the heart of a girl

        with such ever so strange goings on?

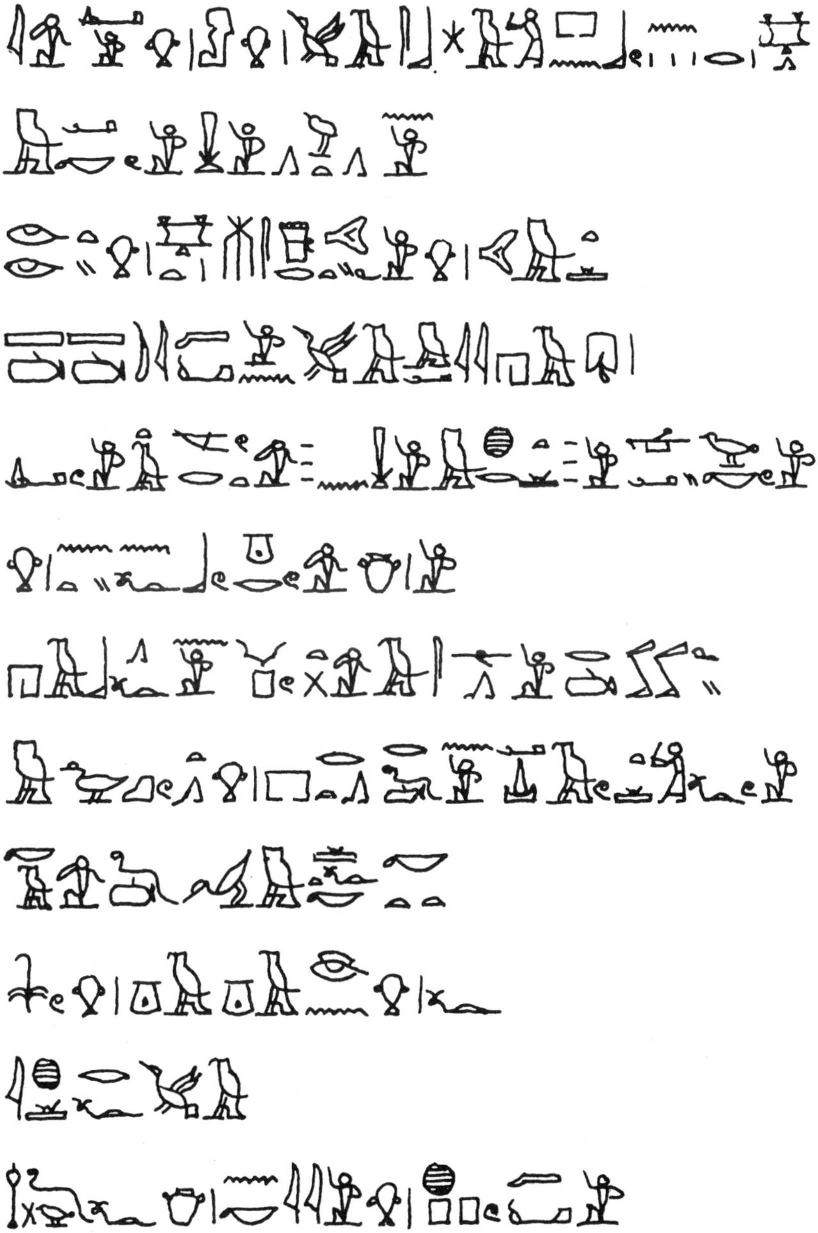

My heart remembers how I once loved you

My heart remembers how I once loved you,
                    as I sit with my hair half done,
And I'm out running, looking for you,
                    searching for you with my hair down!

If I ever get back, I'll weave
                    an intricate hairdo down to my toes.
Love, there's so much time now to finish . . .

Fishing with a draw net

ACKNOWLEDGMENTS

For assistance of many kinds I wish to thank the Egyptologists of the Oriental Institute of the University of Chicago: Professors Klaus Baer, Edward F. Wente, Charles F. Nims, George R. Hughes, and John A. Wilson. I am also grateful to the Department of Health, Education, and Welfare for a fellowship awarded through the National Endowment for the Humanities and to the officers of Roosevelt University for the Research Fellowship which enabled me to complete the book.

115

SOURCES OF THE PAINTINGS

ALL the paintings reproduced here are from Nina M. Davies and A. H. Gardiner, *Ancient Egyptian Paintings*, 3 vols. (Chicago: University of Chicago Press, 1936); plate numbers in the following list refer to this publication. The photographs of the paintings are courtesy of the Oriental Institute, University of Chicago.

Title page: A procession of geese. Pl. I. Medûm, tomb of Itet; reign of Snofru, Dynasty IV, about 2700 B.C. Cairo Museum no. 136E.

Page 4: A nobleman in the cool of his garden. Pl. LXXXVII. Thebes, tomb of Userhēt, no. 51, right-hand end of hall; reign of Sethos I, Dynasty XIX, 1313–1292 B.C.

Page 19: Vintagers and bird catchers. Pl. XLVIII. Thebes, tomb of Nakht, no. 52, back wall of hall, right-hand portion; reign of Tuthmosis IV(?), Dynasty XVIII, 1420–1411 B.C.

Page 23: Singers and dancers. Pl. LXX. Theban tomb painting; reign of Tuthmosis IV or Amenophis III, Dynasty XVIII, 1420–1375 B.C.

Page 34: A pool in a garden. Pl. LXIX. British Museum, no. 37983, from an unlocated tomb at Thebes; reign of Tuthmosis IV or Amenophis III, Dynasty XVIII, 1420–1375 B.C.

Page 49: Guests at a feast. Pl. LXI. Thebes, tomb of Nebamūn and Ipuky, no. 181, front wall of hall, left-hand portion; reign of Amenophis III, Dynasty XVIII, 1411–1375 B.C.

Page 52: Girls bringing fruit and flowers. Pl. LII. Thebes, tomb of Menna, no. 69, front wall of hall, right-hand portion. Reign of Tuthmosis IV(?), Dynasty XVIII, 1420–1411 B.C.

Page 64: Birds in an acacia tree. Pl. IX. Beni-Hasan, tomb of Khnemhotpe, no. 3, top of back wall, main chamber; reign of Amenemmes II or Sesostris II, Dynasty XII, about 1920–1900 B.C.

Page 75: Craftsmen at work. Pl. LXII. Thebes, tomb of Nebamūn and Ipuky, no. 181, front wall of hall, right-hand portion; reign of Amenophis III, Dynasty XVIII, 1411–1375 B.C.

Page 78: Horses and mules at the harvest field. Pl. LXVIII. British Museum, no. 37982, from an unlocated tomb at Thebes; reign of Tuthmosis IV or Amenophis III, Dynasty XVIII, 1420–1375 B.C.

Page 82: Men gathering figs. Pl. VII. Beni-Hasan, tomb of Khnemhotpe, no. 3, main chamber, front wall, left-hand portion; reign of Amenemmes II or Sesostris II, Dynasty XII, about 1920–1900 B.C.

Page 100: Fowling in the marshes. Pl. LXV. Theban tomb painting; reign of Tuthmosis IV or Amenophis III, Dynasty XVIII, 1420–1375 B.C.

Page 106: Officers of a noble household bringing offerings. Pl. XLIV. Thebes, tomb of Sebekhotpe, no. 63, right-hand wall of passage, inner end; reign of Tuthmosis IV, Dynasty XVIII, 1420–1411 B.C.

Page 114: Fishing with a draw net. Pl. XCVI. Thebes, tomb of Ipy, no. 217, front wall of hall, right-hand portion; reign of Ramesses II, Dynasty XIX, 1292–1225 B.C.

INDEX

Oh, I'm bound downstream on the Memphis ferry, 71
Oh, might I speed you on toward your love, 79
Once more you pass her house, deep in thought, 13

Palm trees, heavy with dates, 36

Send him back hard by your lady's small window, 6
So there's love's country nest, 74

The pomegranate bush raises its voice, 83
The voice of the swallow, flittering, calls to me, 108
The wild goose bursts into flight, then settles, 104

Voice of the wild goose crying, 102

What heaven it would be, 107
When her little sycamore, petite, begins to speak, 86
When I hold my love close, 25
When the fig feels called to speak its mind, 85
When we kiss, and her warm lips half open, 26
Whenever I leave you, I go out of breath, 105
Why, just now, must you question your heart, 9

Your love, dear man, is as lovely to me, 18

This is its outcome.

Faithfully rendered from beginning to end

as found in writing.

Done by the scribe,

J.F.